K. Srilata

Footnotes to the Mahabharata

context

Published by Context, an imprint of Westland Books, a division of Nasadiya Technologies Private Limited, in 2025

No. 269/2B, First Floor, 'Irai Arul', Vimalraj Street, Nethaji Nagar, Alapakkam Main Road, Maduravoyal, Chennai 600095

ISBN: 9789360450045

10 9 8 7 6 5 4 3 2

Typeset by Jojy Philip
Printed at Thomson Press (India) Ltd

Footnotes to the Mahabharata

K. Srilata is a poet, fiction writer, translator and academic. Her books include the critically acclaimed *This Kind of Child: The 'Disability' Story* (Westland) and six collections of poetry, the most recent of which, *Three Women in a Single-Room House*, was published by Sahitya Akademi. Srilata has also co-edited the anthologies *The Rapids of a Great River: The Penguin Book of Tamil Poetry, Short Fiction from South India, All the Worlds Between: A Collaborative Poetry Project Between India and Ireland* and *Lifescapes: Interviews with Contemporary Women Writers from Tamilnadu.* Her novel *Table for Four* was long-listed in 2009 for the Man Asian Literary Prize. Her published translations include the works of the Tamil writers Vatsala and Salma. Srilata's poems have been widely anthologised and feature in collections such as *The Bloodaxe Book of Contemporary Indian Poets, The Penguin Book of Indian Poets, The HarperCollins Book of English Poetry* and *A Poem a Day.*

Srilata was awarded the Fulbright fellowship, the Charles Wallace fellowship and a foundation project by the India Foundation for the Arts. She has been writer in residence at the University of Stirling, Scotland, at the Yeonhui Art Space, Seoul and at Sangam House, India. As part of a Feminist Poets' Summit project, Srilata was commissioned by the Goethe-Institut Chennai in cooperation with the Chennai Photo Biennale to write poetry. Her poems have been translated into Tamil, Hindi and Korean.

Formerly a Professor of Literature at IIT Madras, Srilata has taught courses and workshops in Creative Writing at various institutes and universities including the Chennai Mathematical Institute and Ahmedabad University. She is currently Visiting Professor at Shiv Nadar University, Chennai.

Srilata is the Project Coordinator of the Foundation Project implemented by India Foundation for the Arts (IFA) under the Arts Practice programme, made possible with support from Sony Pictures Entertainment Fund.

For the ones who turn footnotes into stories

Contents

No Trunk to This Textual Tree

The Mahabharata

Read simply, the Mahabharata is the story of a family dispute over kingdom and property that leads to a catastrophic war. It is this story that is told in *Jaya* (Victory), essentially a poem about a king winning a battle. As the scholar Irawati Karve argues, it is likely that the poem was sung by bards at the royal court, and also by wandering minstrels. The narrators of this story are believed to have been a class of people known as suta—illegitimate offspring of the Kshatriyas who played various roles at the royal court. The sutas were also wandering storytellers. Karve cites the Mahabharata scholar V.S. Sukthankar, who argues that the narration of the Mahabharata was, at one point in time, taken over by a Brahmin clan named Bhrigu, who added stories of their own to it.[1]

In the Sanskrit version attributed to Vyasa, the version which many consider canonical, the epic is a narrative

---

[1] Irawati Karve, *Yuganta: The End of an Epoch* (Hyderabad: Disha (Orient Longman), 1991).

pastiche made up of prose passages and 1,00,000 shlokas—each shloka working like a couplet. A chapter or adhyaya consists of several shlokas and several adhyayas, in turn, form a parva. The Mahabharata is popularly understood to have eighteen parvas, though even this is open to debate. It is nearly impossible to ascertain how many manuscripts of the Mahabharata are in existence and, in fact, no complete list of these manuscripts has ever been compiled. The Bhandarkar Oriental Research Institute (BORI) undertook the project of collating and unifying various versions of the text, but even that is probably doomed to be an incomplete project. The parvas have been handed down separately or in small groups, at least in the oldest Mahabharata manuscripts.

The Mahabharata contains stories within stories but somehow, magically, neither the various threads nor the main plot are ever lost. A story slips out of view only to reappear at another point in the narrative. The stories also have multiple narrators. The frame tale begins with sage Shaunaka, who is engaged in the performance of a twelve-year-long ritual which proves to be a magnet for storytellers. Ugrashrava, the son of the famous suta storyteller Lomaharshana, appears on the scene one day and is greeted with cries of joy. Everyone implores him to tell the story of his travels. Ugrashrava describes his visits to various sacred places and narrates the story of King Janamejaya of Hastinapura and the Naga sacrifice he had performed to avenge the death of his father King Parikshita. In this story embedded within the frame tale, the sage Vyasa persuades Janamejaya to give up his desire for revenge. That is when Janamejaya expresses his wish to hear stories of his ancestors. Vyasa asks his disciple Vaishampayana to tell Janamejaya the story of his ancestors, and from here on, it is Vaishampayana who becomes the narrator.

There is another change of narrator during the Kurukshetra war. The blind king Dhritarashtra desires to know what is going on in the battlefield. It is the suta Sanjaya who gives him an eyewitness account. Hence, that portion of the Mahabharata is narrated by Sanjaya. As Karwe points out, what we have therefore is 'the first narrator Ugrashrava who tells the story up to a point, and then tells it as told by the second narrator Vaishampayana who in his turn is the chief narrator up to a point and then tells it as told by the third narrator Sanjaya and after the battle portion resumes it.' In addition, there are a number of other minor narrators who, from time to time, narrate stories which are not so important. Vyasa himself is supposed to have played a part in the events and witnesses many of them. He passes on the stories to his disciples, one of whom is Vaishampayana and the other Jaimini. The versions narrated by Vaishampayana differ from Jaimini's going by the fragment which remains of the latter.

The Mahabharata is a masterpiece in terms of design and structure. What happens in one parva foreshadows or is otherwise connected to what happens in another one. Tales are nested within each other, and so the work of laying out the backstories is complicated. The tales in the Mahabharata call for retrospective sense-making, a piecing together of one enormous jigsaw puzzle.

As Norman Brown points out in his foreword to Irawati Karve's *Yuganta*, the characters in the Mahabharata, unlike those in the Ramayana, are emotionally complex beings. They are shades of grey, each one of them. Even Duryodhana, who we think of as the villain, has reasons to act as he does. Krishna, despite his divinity, is a master manipulator. Draupadi is often arrogant and Gandhari acts out of anger and resentment when she voluntarily blindfolds herself. The emotional complexity of the epic's characters perhaps explains its many retellings. Shaped by generations of poets and storytellers, the Mahabharata lives and breathes in these retellings. Its constantly evolving nature means that you can never hope to catch up with it fully. Just when you think you are all caught up, a new tale or an old one differently told surfaces. Each person knows the Mahabharata differently and even this individual knowing changes through time. To assume finiteness of knowing is therefore both pointless and dangerous. Some Mahabharata stories—especially those that are later interpolations such as the Tamil *Bharatham*, for instance, or the Bhil Mahabharata or the Alli ballad—are not known beyond their places of origin. Some may even be in danger of extinction. If you are lucky, you may discover some of them by accident or serendipity. Versions of the Mahabharata's tales may oftentimes contradict each another, but that is par for the course and only makes for a richer interpretative field.

The scholar Wendy Doniger points out that the Mahabharata marks the transition from the corpus of Sanskrit texts known as shruti—the Vedic canon of texts dating back to roughly 1500 BCE which are unalterable—to those known as smriti, which is 'the human tradition, constantly revised, the "remembered texts" of human authorship, texts that could be altered.' [2]

There is, of course, a strong human impulse to collate and 'unify' the multiple versions of the text, to tidy it all up, to arrive at a sense of that one text. Between the years 1919 and 1966, BORI produced what is known as the critical edition of the Mahabharata, an attempt to unify the text across its various regional variations.[3] The editor of the 1933 first critical BORI edition, V.S. Sukthankar,

---

[2] Wendy Doniger, 'The Mahabharata: A Text for All Seasons', Foreword to Carole Satyamurti's *Mahabharata: A Modern Retelling* (New York: Norton, 2015), p. xxii.

[3] V.S. Sukthankar in his 'Prologomena' (critical edition of the Ādiparvan, Book I of the Mahabharata), points out that the need for a critical or 'correct' edition of the Mahabharata had been felt by Sanskritists for over half a century before the BORI critical edition came out, but that it was voiced for the first time by Professor M. Winternitz, at the XIth International Congress of Orientalists, held at Paris, in 1897. Winternitz proposed the foundation of a Sanskrit Epic Text Society. His proposal was laid before the next session of the Oriental Congress (XIIth), held in Rome (1899), but was received with much scepticism. After the war, the BORI commenced work on the project. It was not until 1933, however, that the first critical edition was published.

argues that 'since not even the seemingly most irrelevant line or stanza, actually found in a Mahābhārata manuscript collated for the edition, is on any account omitted', this edition would be more complete than any previous one ('Prolegomena', p. 4).[4] Sukthankar claims that the first critical BORI edition would prove to be a 'veritable thesaurus of the Mahābhārata tradition'.

Even as one admires the BORI critical edition's ambitious scope and the extensive and meticulous scholarship that has gone into its making, one is left with the niggling sense that it is impossible to tidy up the messiness of the Mahabharata and that in fact, this messiness is actually rather delightful. The impulse to modify a tale or to create a new one, to add yet another interpretation or twist, has driven many poets, scholars and writers to retell the Mahabharata, to work with tales or aspects of the text which have either appealed to them or have got under their skin for some reason.

One must make peace with the fact that looking for an urtext, the 'original' Mahabharata from which the others flowed, is akin to looking for a needle in a haystack. In fact, there is no such thing as the 'original' Mahabharata, only a text which some have constructed as canonical and may, therefore, be received as the 'original' by many. As Doniger argues so persuasively: '... there is no trunk to this textual tree, no pristine *Ur-Mahabharata* for scholars

---

[4] V.S. Sukthankar, *The Mahabharata* ('Adiparvan'), Volume 1 (Pune: Bhandarkar Oriental Research Institute, 1933).

to isolate from a mass of corrupted texts; if it is a tree at all, it is a banyan, which must have an original root but sends down so many subsequent roots from its branches (other variants) that one can no longer tell which was the original.' [5]

In so many ways, what we are trained to think of as the 'original' Mahabharata anticipates its own retelling. And in the end, it is that openness, the space for yet another teller to jump in, which makes the Mahabharata such a happening text.

I have often asked myself what witchcraft it was that drew me to this long, hyper-linked, circular text. In my own eyes, I was an unlikely candidate. I was not a Sanskritist and the version of the text which enjoys canonical status is in Sanskrit. In the decades leading up to this book, I had not actively thought about or studied the Mahabharata. But like many children of the seventies and eighties, I had grown up on a diet of racially coded Amar Chitra Kathas. My mother and grandmother had told me stories of the Ramayana and the Mahabharata, so I knew who was who and who did what and to whom. I remember being enchanted by these stories, by the comic books' pictorial representation of characters. I knew the gods (they were all fair-skinned), I knew the Rakshasas (they were all dark-skinned), I knew the

---

[5] Wendy Doniger, 'How to Escape the Curse', a review of John Smith's translation of the Mahabharata in the *London Review of Books*, Vol. 31, No.19 (8 October 2009).

chaste and impossibly beautiful women, I knew the brave and handsome warriors. The epics held me then, to the extent any good black-and-white story holds children, and very often for troubling reasons. But as I grew older, that childhood enchantment shattered and was slowly but surely crowded out by other concerns. By the time I got to university, I was knee-deep in feminist theory and was writing my thesis on the Periyarite anti-caste movement in Tamil Nadu. So much about the Ramayana and the Mahabharata had started to feel problematic. The gods, the sages and the Kshatriyas in these stories, and their various shenanigans, felt suspect. I knew, of course, of the existence of retellings and variations of the epics, but I did not have the time or the mind space for them. What followed was a two-and-a-half-decades- long immersion in academia and motherhood, neither of which led me to an engagement with the epics, except briefly, when I tried (and failed) to get my children interested in them. But the Mahabharata re-entered my life serendipitously after a long absence. I was dusting my bookshelves one day when I discovered a brand-new copy of *Parva*, S.L. Bhyrappa's Kannada novel based on the Mahabharata and translated into English by Raghavendra Rao. I had no recollection of when and where I had bought it or even what impulse it was that had prompted the purchase. I flipped it open. Before I knew it, I was lost in its pages, consumed by the story Bhyrappa was telling, and the dusting was abandoned. Bhyrappa's version of the epic led me to others and those, in turn, to yet others. The epic had mysteriously found its way to me, the proverbial message in a bottle. As I followed fault lines, cracks and fissures in the Mahabharata corpus, what stood out for me were the women's stories. Some of these, like Kunti's and Draupadi's, had already been the subject of quirky and unorthodox tellings, and I have built on the foundations of these.[6] Others, such as Alli's, were marked by silences and gaps which serve as the edifice for my poems.

The five poetic sequences which constitute this collection explore the lives of Alli, Hidimbi, Draupadi, Gandhari and Kunti. I have deliberately chosen to open with Alli—a character exclusive to the Tamil, Dravidian tradition, not on the map of the mainstream Mahabharata. Alli is followed by Hidimbi who, with a few notable exceptions and despite the temple dedicated to her in Manali, has remained but a footnote in the larger narrative about the Pandavas.

It was happenstance that when I started work on this manuscript, I had been experimenting with haikai forms—such as the haiku, the senryu and the haibun. The haikai tradition has seeped into the writing of some poems. While a few open or conclude with a haiku, some others have the haiku running side by side with the main text of the poem. The dramatic monologue with its silent listener—in this case, the figure of the Sakhi or the

---

[6] Listed in the 'Readings and References' section is a personal roadmap of these tellings, texts which have served as source material for the poems.

heroine's friend—is a form I have used almost throughout. The Sakhi listens in silence as the heroine speaks. This, of course, is mandated by the form. But even as she remains in the shadows, the Sakhi has a crucial role to perform. For the heroine to reveal herself fully, the Sakhi's presence is necessary.

Moving away from Western poetry-titling practices, I have drawn on the titling tradition of Tamil Sangam Agananuru and Purananuru poetry, in which titles declare upfront who is speaking to whom. A typical example would be 'What the Heroine Said to Her Friend'.

This approach to titling seemed especially suited for the dramatic monologue. Not only does it serve the pragmatic function of making clear who is speaking to whom, it also carries a certain poetic charge.

The section titled 'Source Tales' offers a brief overview of the tales and the source texts which seeded the poems. This is meant for readers who would like some backstory. My attempt has been to cite and attribute wherever I can, but the 'tangled aerial roots' of these poems and how they made their way to the page makes that impossible at times. I hope I will be forgiven these lapses.

I think of these sequences as little boats that have set off from various motherships. Read them as part of an endless chain of refracted Mahabharata tales, tales that extend, amplify and riff off each other.

In Ink Invisible

Beloved
of storytellers   of poets
of listeners   of readers

no beginning   no end
tales hiding inside tales

waiting in the wings
shadow tales   opposite tales
tales unequal   off the record

What of the voices Vyasa unheard,
Vaisampayana and Ugrashrava unrecited,
and Janamejaya unknew?

What of the upaparvas skipped over,
the ones Ganesha never wrote,
the ones in ink invisible?

ALLI

Says the Pandyan King to the Queen

The Daughter We Will Never Have

She reaches for the moon incandescent—
the daughter we will never have,
and your eyes as they follow her are liquid love—

last night's dream
tremulous as a bird wing.

Says the Pandyan Queen to the King

Month After Month

ebbs
  and flows
    month after month
  my blood river

month after month
  she drowns
    our daughter
  the one we will never have.

Says the Pandyan King to the Queen

So Silken Our Daughter's Skin

Even the water lily
within whose petals
I found her,
is put to shame.
So silken, our daughter's skin.
Run your fingers over it. See for yourself!

Says the Pandyan King to the Queen

More Son Than Daughter

'You raised this daughter of ours
to be a warrior
and now she won't look at a man,'
you complain.
But isn't it thanks to her—
more son than daughter—
that we have our kingdom back?
Quit complaining and be glad.
Our Alli can do better than a man.

Says One Beggar Woman to Another on the Streets of Madurai

Listen, Mother,
Pay no heed
to wagging tongues.
Our Alli has a tender heart.
Why, just yesterday
she nursed a fledgling
which the storm
had forced out of its nest.

Her fierceness, Mother,
is reserved for the wicked.
With the likes of us,
she is most gentle.
Go on. Don't be afraid!
Knock on the palace gates,
ask to see her.

wilderness—
the scent of mogras
escapes notice

Says the Innkeeper to Arjuna

Our Alli Has Never Needed a Man

'I am yet to meet a woman immune to my charms.
Your Alli, I am sure, is no different,' you say.
Stranger, you will soon be eating your words.
Full red lips   slender waist
raisin eyes   skin softer than jasmine
fearless to a fault   warrior beyond compare.
Our Alli has never needed a man.

Says Arjuna to Krishna

Come What May

Come what may, I must have Alli.
You know how it is with me and women I fancy.
Conquer them, I must
or I can't rest in peace.
Let's go to her dressed as women.
Let's trick Madurai's warrior queen.

Says Alli to Her Friend

I Have Been Tricked

Turns out it was a man all along!
Thozhi, I have been tricked.
Scratches,
bite marks,
hair in disarray,
vermilion smudged.
Thozhi, I am undone.

Even this chatterbox of a parrot
has fallen silent
and looks at me as if to ask:
'Are you alright?'

What the Men Said About Alli

This is what they all said—
respectable men,
pious men,
men with beards,
men with smirks.
This is what they all said behind her back
on the streets of Madurai.

Look how she has fallen—our arrogant Alli—they said.
We saw this coming, they said.
She who thought she was as good as a man
is just another of Arjuna's wives now, they said.
This is what happens to women
who grow too big for their boots, they said.
In the end, our Alli was easy to seduce.

Says Alli to Her Friend

I Tried Every Trick

Wild elephants, snakes,
crushed seeds of arali—
Thozhi, I tried every trick in the book
but that wily Arjuna survived it all.
And when I offered him to the goddess
as a sacrifice,
thinking that would put an end to it,
she turned up her nose and declared,
'Alli, you can't pass off something you don't want
as an offering to me.'

Says Alli to Her Friend

It's to Myself I Belong

'Might as well accept your lot, you say,
make peace with things.
Learn to be a woman.
Give up this foolishness.
Alli, of what use are bows and arrows
when Arjuna himself is yours?'

Whose side are you on, Thozhi,
his or mine?
It's to myself I belong,
not to men who take me against my will.
And this has nothing to do with Kama.
So don't sell me that story.
Thozhi, after all that has come to pass,
do you really expect me
to become one of Arjuna's wives?

dark night
the crescent moon
still sharp as a sickle

HIDIMBI

They Say

that I give off a certain animal smell,
that I am too much, too loud,
too dark, too muscular,
                                        too wanton,
that I am a sorceress and a thief,
that if only I had thought to look in the mirror,
I wouldn't have dreamt of a Kshatriya man,
that a Rakshasi like me should know better,
that good men should guard themselves
against creatures like me,
that trapped by the likes of us,
                              they lose themselves.

palash flowers—
biting my lips
until they turn red

The Day Bhima Brought Me Home

Mother Kunti said, her voice a murmuring stream,
'May good things come your way, Daughter.'
She is a gracious woman, Mother Kunti,
a woman who bestows blessings
with practised ease
and calls everyone 'daughter'.
Even the shock in her eyes
when she first beheld me
was but a flicker.

When I First Met Yudhishtira

In a gentle voice, he said,
'I should welcome you with a gift,
but alas, I have nothing to give.
Forgive me, Hidimbi.'
But when I touched his feet
and sought his blessings,
how he jumped—
that righteous brother-in-law of mine!

Beloved

Much was said
on the morning they left.
'We can't possibly take her with us.'
'It is unthinkable. Bhima, be reasonable.'
'Son, your time with her was borrowed time.'
'In time, there will be other women.'
'You can always visit her when the fancy takes you.'
'She will soon be a distant memory. Take my word for it.'
'A warrior must know when to move on. Don't be such a
crybaby.'

'But she is with child.'

'Mother knows she is.'
'She served us well.'
'She wasn't bad for a Rakshasi.'
'May you be blessed with a son, Hidimbi.'

On the morning they left,
much was said
but I had ears

only for that one word
of Bhima's:
'Beloved.'

through my heart-bird
the arrow
of that word

Prison House

Even as the solitary heron
drying herself,
shakes off water droplets,
I yearn to shake off my longing for Bhima.
But alas, love is a prison house
and I am in for life.

This Thought That We Might Never Again Meet

Lonely as a swan without her mate,
this thought, Bhima,
that we might never again meet
or that if we do, years later,
the parts of us which have grown
in the absence of the other,
and those which have decayed,
will greet each other as strangers.

Says Ghatotkacha to Hidimbi

Mother, They Bully Me So!

You ask why I no longer play with them
but Mother, they bully me so!

'Where's your father? Tell us!'
'What's his name?'
'What sort of name is Bhima?'
'So, if he is a warrior, why did he run away?'
'Afraid of us Rakshasas, was he?'
'How come he never comes to see you?'
'Don't lie to us, Ghatotkacha.'
'Tell us, whose son are you really?'

You ask why
I no longer play with them
but Mother, they bully me so!

Says Hidimbi to Ghatotkacha

Tell Them Bhimasena Is No Ordinary Man

Son, the next time those bullies come for you,
tell them just who your father is.
Tell them Bhimasena is no ordinary man,
that this son of the mighty wind god
has the strength of a thousand bulls
and the heart of a lion.

Tell them, too, of the love
your heart holds for him and his for you,
vaster than the sky, tender as palm fruit.

None Save Me to Grieve Your Death

'Ghatotkacha may be the son of Bhima but let's not forget he is a forest-dweller, that he has the nature of a demon. We would have had to kill him some day.'

—Krishna, the protector of dharma

Beloved son,
more radiant than the moon,
mightier than a thousand elephants,
they sent for you
so you could pay for Arjuna's life with yours,
help win a battle not of your making.
You had no idea what the game was, did you?

None, save me, to grieve your death.
None to build you a pyre.
No warrior's farewell for you,
my beloved son, more radiant than the moon.

Says Hidimbi to Herself

Are we but footnotes in the war?

footnote:
an addition
a piece of information printed at the bottom of a page,
also, a thing that is additional, less important
or relatively subordinate.

DRAUPADI

Says Draupadi to Sakhi Nitambini

The Girl Who Wasn't Invited

An afterthought of fire,
I was the daughter they hadn't asked for,
didn't know what to do with.

This girl of yours will change the course of history.

I felt it all in my infant bones—
the un-invitation,
my mother's slight stiffening,
my father's embrace, polite and uncertain.
I felt it early, Nitambini—
the weariness of being Draupadi.

Says Queen Prishati to King Drupad

She Sent for a Quill

That daughter of yours
is a strange one.
She cares neither for jewels nor clothes.
All day long, she sits gazing out the window,
lost in thought.
Dressed in the dullest of garments,
jasmine buds her only jewels,
that daughter of yours—
Why, she is practically an ascetic!
Only the other day, she sent for a quill.
'To write poems with,' she said.
What kind of prince will marry such a girl?

Says Queen Prishati to Draupadi

Put Away Your Quill

Put away that parchment,
put away your quill.
Scriptures and poems
are of no use to women.
Cast aside your coarse garments.
Drape yourself in these silks
softer than deerskin.
Try on these pearls,
more lustrous than the moon.

Put away that parchment.
Put away your quill.
Mark my words, Daughter,
you won't go far
with this life of the mind.

Says Draupadi to Sakhi Nitambini

My Heart Will Go Where It Pleases

'What business has Krishnaa with Krishna?'[1]
you tease when I ask you what he is like.
'You are but a slip of a girl
unschooled in the ways of love
and he, why, he has sixteen thousand gopis in a spin!
You haven't a chance, Draupadi.'

But Sakhi, there isn't a stable in the world
that can hold this runaway colt—
my heart will go where it pleases.
There isn't a thing I can do.
Don't you get it?

Says Draupadi to Sakhi Nitambini

Hardest Are Those Nights

Hardest are those nights
when the air grips
in its chokehold
the scent of blue lilies,
for it makes me think of Krishna.
I can no longer bear it, Sakhi.
Is there really no cure for love?

Says Draupadi to Sakhi Nitambini

Am I Not Crazy Already?

'Be my eyes
and tell me what Krishna is like,'
I implore.
And you say you daren't risk it.
'What if I do and you lose your mind?' you ask,
refusing to humour me.
But Sakhi, am I not crazy already?
Look! It is the third night in a row,
that Mother has found me
sleepwalking through the garden
muttering over and over,
'Are his feet really like lotus buds?'

Says Sakhi Nitambini to Draupadi

I Wasn't Born Yesterday!

The instant you wake up,
you recite Krishna's name
and when I tease you about it,
you claim at first that it is Nilmani[2]
and not you who is calling out to him.
When I persist, you respond slyly,
'But when I said "Krishna", I really meant Nilmani.'
Princess, I wasn't born yesterday.
Do you really think
I will fall for sophistry and word play?

Says Sakhi Nitambini to Draupadi

It's Not My Fault, You Say

'It's not my fault,' you say,
'that he was named Nilmani.'
'Blame the court poet
who brought me that list of names.'
'That my eyes came to rest on "Nilmani"
was sheer happenstance.'
'How was I to know
that it was a synonym for Krishna?'
Draupadi, you have no idea
how lousy you are at lying!

Says Draupadi to Sakhi Nitambini on First Spotting Arjuna

Sakhi, quick, come take a look at this mendicant
more handsome than the god of love,
his chest broader than the base of a mountain,
his skin the hue of rain clouds,
his eyes lotuses freshly bloomed,
and tell me if he isn't
the spitting image of Krishna.
Or is that just my eyes playing tricks?

Says Draupadi to Krishna
Don't Think You Can Fob Me Off

All day long have I spent
weaving this garland of jasmine
and you refuse it.

'Give it to Arjuna,' you say,
offering your friendship as a sop.
'Makes no difference
who wears the garland,' you say.
'After all, as the whole world knows
Arjuna is a part of me.'

I am no fool, Krishna.
Don't think you can fob me off
with your tall tales!

Says Sakhi Nitambini to Draupadi

Haven't You Heard That Old Story?

Draupadi, haven't you heard that old story?
This lotus-eyed suitor of yours
once split with his arrow
a mustard seed balanced on a hill fort.
So, stop saying: *This Arjuna isn't a patch on my Krishna*
and go find me a woman luckier than you.

Says Draupadi to Sakhi Nitambini

Who Are They Calling a Whore?

The scriptures proclaim,
'You are not your body.'
If Draupadi's body isn't Draupadi,
then who are they calling a whore?

Says Draupadi to Sakhi Nitambini

The Thorn of His Question

'As different as sugar and salt,
as unalike as rivers and mountains,
my brothers and I.
How do you propose to handle us?'
asks Yudhishtira.

hidden amidst roses
the thorn
of his question

Says Draupadi to Sakhi Nitambini

I Am a Simple Man

Do you know what the mighty Bhima
said to me on our wedding night?
'I am a simple man, Draupadi, but quick to anger.
All I expect is the pleasure of your company
when I seek it.
Of my love for food, you have no doubt heard.
Bear these things in mind, Draupadi
and you will have nothing to fear.'

radiant moon—
behind it
the stealth of darkness

Says Draupadi to Sakhi Nitambini

This Thread Is Fraying

'Like the thread
used to string jasmine
is your daughter,'
said Krishna to my father.
'She will keep the five together.'
But this thread, dear Sakhi,
is fraying,
coming undone,
one knot at a time.

Says Draupadi to Sakhi Nitambini

What Do I Do with a Man Like This?

He insists I go to him every night,
that jealous Bhima.
It's always some excuse or the other:
I am unwell. My stomach hurts. You fed me too much.
Make me some kashaya. Massage my feet, they hurt so!
Stay with me until I fall asleep.
Don't go. What's the hurry?
And all the while, Sakhi,
I am thinking of Yudhisthtira
whose turn it is with me.
Surely he must wonder what's keeping me?
This Bhima, Sakhi, is worse than a child.
When I tell him
I really must be on my way,
he retreats into a sulk.
'Let me not hold you back, Draupadi,'
he says with a heavy sigh.
'Clearly, your heart is with Yudhishtira.
I am nothing to you.
I will go to Hidimbi.
She is the only one who loves me.'
Sakhi, what do I do with a man like this?

Says Draupadi to Bhima

Is This Fair?

Knowing fully that I cannot
spend the night with you,
that this year I am Yudhishtira's,
you still say:
Massage my feet.
Stay.
My stomach hurts,
make me some kashaya.
If you leave me now,
I will go to Hidimbi.

When I cite that contract
which binds us all,
and plead helplessness,
you cry out like a petulant child,
'Damn that contract!
I have had enough
of all your excuses!'
When I say I love you
as much as I do the others,

you stamp your feet and declare petulantly,
'No, you don't!
Pack my bags, Draupadi.
I am going to Hidimbi
this very minute!'
Bhima, tell me, is this fair?

Says Draupadi to Kunti

I Have Walked the Tightrope of Your Words

'Whatever it is you have brought home,
share it equally with your brothers,'
you said to Arjuna
without so much as turning around.
I have walked the tightrope
of your words, Mother,
lived them to the letter,
my time and my heart
carved in five.
And yet, tonight,
at the mere sight of the crescent moon,
I am beset
by an out-of-turn longing.
What do I do, Mother?

Says Draupadi to Sakhi Nitambini

I Haven't a Chance

Sakhi, that husband of mine
has brought home another wife.
I know in my heart
that I haven't a chance,
for Subhadra is fresh
as a bud of jasmine.
No wonder Arjuna
can't take his eyes off her!

Says Draupadi to Sakhi Nitambini

Subhadra's Feet

Smaller than a child's,
more dainty than a lotus,
softer even than butter,
Subhadra's feet.
No wonder she has Arjuna's heart!

Says Draupadi to Sakhi Nitambini

Karna's Words

Sakhi, like peas in a pod,
Karna's feet and Mother Kunti's,
that second toe longer than the first,
the little toe a shy jasmine bud.
Can I be blamed, Sakhi,
for mixing them up?

But when I bent down
and touched his feet instead of hers,
Karna's words were sharper than a lance:
'Behold the queen of Hastinapur
touching the feet of a mere charioteer!
Now what will her five husbands say?'

hard to tell
one from the other
the call of a mocking bird

Says Draupadi to Sakhi Nitambini

I Burn and Burn

Sakhi, do you know what Karna said of me?
'Even to sip water
offered by a woman such as her
is to lose one's dharma.
She ought to know that better than anyone else,
this woman who fancies herself a scholar.'

Sakhi, I burn and burn,
no water to put out this fire.

Says Draupadi to Sakhi Nitambini

I Will Not Forget the Summoning

Sakhi, for as long as I live,
I will not forget the summoning,
  the burn of Pratikami's words,
  'King Duryodhana commands that you go to him.'
And me, in a single garment.
O, the shame of it, Sakhi!

Between my legs,
that slow drip of blood.
  Have mercy!
  Let go!

Duhshasan's laughter,
'Forget your modesty,
come to us!'
Have mercy!
Let go!

Who is this woman whose sari is slipping,
this woman trying to cover her breasts?
Whose voice is it that I hear?

Sharper than knives, their eyes,
their crawling hands.

Look! Her sari is slipping!
Cover your breasts, Draupadi, do something, quick!

running
running from
running between
slow drip of blood
Whose body is that?
    Have mercy!
    Let go!

Who is this woman whose sari is slipping,
this woman trying to cover her breasts,
running in a body no longer her own?

O, where did she go—that other woman,
the one who sat in the quiet of her room
reading and writing?
That girl-woman from before,

where did she go?
You used to know her, Sakhi.
That girl-woman from before,
where did she go?

GANDHARI

Says Gandhari to Her Friend

Can My Eyes Take the Light?

in last night's dream
hill-blue
like the arch of an eyebrow

Sakhi, I remember the day as if it were yesterday.
I was watching a peacock,
the outspread of his wings,
the blue glisten of his neck
in the singing rain,
when you came running.

'Princess, you have been deceived. The man is blind!'
Only that morning, you had lined my eyes with kohl.
'A princess without kohl in her eyes is no princess.'
Sakhi, I did what good wives do. I walked in his shoes.
'And what if you had been blind, Princess? Would he
have walked in yours?'

A hundred sons I bore him and one daughter.
And I know not their faces, dear Sakhi,

except what I see with my fingers,
but mine, unlike his, is an imperfect seeing,
since I came to it so late.
My fingers do not see the blue-hued hills,
nor do my ears pick up
the tilt of Duryodhana's head.
And to think, Sakhi, that he sees it all,
the way I did that peacock singing in the rain.
O, there are days when I long to undo
the knot just to know Dussala's smile.
    'But what keeps you, Princess?'
I wonder, Sakhi, can my eyes take the light?
Will the world take colour and shape?
Will you line my eyes with kohl again?
Sakhi, will I see even less than I do now?

Says Gandhari to Her Friend

The More I Burned

watching
yesterday's chimera
my eyes unseeing

Sakhi, perhaps you were right
when you said:
'Watch out, Princess!
Don't become your own jailor.'
But my anger blazed brighter
than the noon sun.
The more I burned,
the taller grew the prison walls.
'This is too heavy a burden for me to bear, Gandhari,
won't you relent?' says Dhritarashtra.
But these walls—
the longer I stay within
the more impossible are they to scale.

Says Gandhari to Her Friend

My Daughter's Face

new moon to full moon
circling
the same question

This much I can tell, Sakhi:
that my daughter's face
is as round as the moon,
that her eyes are almonds,
and her lips sweet raisins,
that her skin's a rose petal.
Is it true what they say?
Does Dussala really look like me?

Says Gandhari's Friend to Her

Being Girls Together

Remember that young jeweller
from many moons ago?
Remember how
he stared and stared at your face
and we thought him over-bold?

suppressed giggles
all that's left
of our being girls together

Says Gandhari's Friend to Her

Not a Care in the World

Casting your eyes
on spring's first leaves, you said,
'That green ...
how it gladdens my heart.'

We were girls then, the two of us,
with not a care in the world
and all the time for spring.
How far we have strayed!

giving spring a miss
a palette
filled with greys

Says Gandhari's Friend to Her

The Bangles You Threw a Tantrum For

recast
in the eastern sky
yesterday's gold

No pleasure
do my eyes find
in these chambers
where a thousand lamps light
things of joy.
What gladdens me
is that which I see undimmed
in my mind's eye—
the lilt of rubies on the bangles
you threw a tantrum for
and wore as a girl
all those years ago.

Says Gandhari to Her Friend

The Life That Might Have Been Mine

Sakhi, do you remember
the night my mother
found me with him?

'You are a princess
and he, a mere jeweller.
Are you out of your mind?
This is a recipe for disaster,'
she shouted, dragging me away.

And you, Sakhi, added fuel to the fire.
'Didn't I say so, Gandhari? He is no match for you.'
And later, when we were by ourselves,
didn't you say to me:
'Forget him, Gandhari. Just get him out of your mind.
Listen to your mother.'

You will think me mad for saying this
but on bad days

my thoughts turn to him
as sunflowers to sun
and I mourn the life
that might have been mine.

Says Gandhari to Her Friend

Don't Tell Me About Kurukshetra

Sakhi, don't tell me about Kurukshetra,
of the sparrows which rain down from the skies.
Don't tell me of the sun which refuses to show up,
of the tall pyres that will never stop burning.
Don't tell me of bereaved mothers,
of the precise nature of their grief.
Don't tell me who killed my sons
and how they went about their business.
Don't tell me, Sakhi, about the dharma of war.

Says Gandhari to Her Friend

I Bless Them as an Elder Should

After the war is done and dusted,
they come to me, Kunti's five,
and I bless them as an elder should.
'May you live long, Son.'
'May the kingdom prosper.'
'May you and yours be happy.'
'Bless you, Son. Bless you.'
And all the while,
the bile rises in my throat.

Says Gandhari to Her Friend

Grief's Saddest Language

Piercing the palace walls,
Grief's saddest language speaks
in the wordlessness of a mother's dirge.
Wrapped in the shroud
of death's long sleep
is her foot soldier son
and still, the men maintain
that the war was imperative!

KUNTI

Says Kunti to Her Friend

So Claims That Worthless Husband

'I took them in the palace,
I took them in the woods,
Some I took in full view of the world,
some I took clandestinely.
What a hit I was with the maids!
They couldn't have enough of me!
Your maid with the ample hips—
I took her too.'
So claims that worthless husband of mine.
Desert-dry are my eyes, Sakhi,
for these are clearly empty boasts.
But how do I contain this feral cat—
this snicker which will not be suppressed?

Says Kunti

By All Means, Old Man

Certain it will do the trick,
my husband's grandfather
is off to fetch him a new bride.
'Come what may, the Kuru lineage must continue,'
he says in his gruff voice,
'Kunti is clearly not up to it.'

By all means, old man,
buy Pandu another wife.
A new field yields nothing
when ploughed with the same old broken plough.
Any fool will tell you that!

Says Pandu to Kunti

Quick, Give Me a Son

We haven't a minute to lose, Kunti!
Who knows when those herbs and potions will do their work?
Quick, Kunti, conceive a son!
Surely you heard what the messenger said?
What if my brother and his bride get ahead of the game?
The Kuru kingdom could well be their son's.
And I, heirless, forgotten, consigned to dust ...
Doesn't bear thinking about, Kunti.
Quick, conceive a son!
Sleep with a Deva if that's what it takes
but give me a son.
Why, even the sages swear
that there is no shame in *niyoga*.[3]
Quick, Kunti,
do what it takes but give me a son.

Says Pandu to Kunti

Keep Your Thoughts on Me

Like the practised hunter whose eyes
remain always on his prey,
keep your thoughts on me.
The pleasures of the body
are as fleeting as dreams.
They retreat in the blink of an eye.
But our hearts,
our hearts, Kunti, must remain unsullied,
lotus leaves in a pond.

Says Kunti to Her Friend

The Delicious Rogueness of Bodies

It's all very well, Sakhi, for my husband to say:
'The pleasures of the body
are as fleeting as dreams.'
All very well for him to declare
that our hearts must remain unsullied.
Such words roll easily off the tongues
of men like him.
But for me who knows
the delicious rogueness of bodies,
his words are empty
as a pauper's purse.

Says Kunti to Her Friend

Where Maruta Comes From

Where Maruta comes from,
sweet-scented flowers bloom
through the year,
blue-necked peacocks dance day-long,
squirrels grow fat on luscious jackfruit,
rivers never run dry,
and a woman can take any man she wants.
Are you listening, Sakhi?

Says Kunti to Her Friend

Like the Pugmarks of a Wild Animal

Like the pugmarks of a wild animal,
Maruta's impress on me.
And yet, Sakhi,
you stand there saying,
'Forget him. He is not for you.'

Says Kunti to Her Friend

No Ordinary Thief

'In my country,' claims Maruta,
as he draws me to him,
'there are a thousand ways
in which lovers embrace.
Would you like me to teach you?'

In the crush of his arms, Sakhi,
my bangles slip from my wrists.
As for my heart, it is stolen before I know it.
He's no ordinary thief, this Maruta.

Says Kunti to Her Friend

That Which You Warned Me Against

Sakhi, listen,
that which you warned me against
has come to pass.
Water has seeped into this lotus leaf,
my heart is brimming with desire.
And you are still hoping
I will forget him!

Says Kunti to Her Friend

Each Time I See a Tall Man

Each time I see a tall man
I think it's him
and call out his name.
What a fool
I must seem, Sakhi,
to the people of this town!

Says Kunti to Her Friend

The Sweetness of Love

Sakhi, like an ant
that has fallen
into honey,
I drown,
even as I sip
on the sweetness
of love.

Says Kunti to Her Friend

All Day Long

All day long
I think of him
and the day ends
before I am done.
Is there a way, Sakhi,
to stop the sun from setting?

Says Kunti to Her Friend

Our Thoughts Are Vagrant Birds

It's true, Sakhi,
what my husband feared.
Our thoughts are indeed vagrant birds.
Look at mine,
so off course,
so lost in Maruta.

Says Kunti to Her Friend

On a Full Moon Night Such as This

Sakhi, don't you get it?
It was on a full moon night
such as this
that my eyes
beheld him for the last time,
and yet, you stand there
singing this evil moon's praises,
and wonder why I take umbrage.

Endnotes to the Poems

1. This line is borrowed from Chapter Three of Prathibha Ray's *Yajnaseni: The Story of Draupadi.*

2. Draupadi's pet blackbird. The words 'Nilmani' and 'Krishna' both mean that which is blue-hued. 'Nilmani' literally means 'blue gemstone' whereas 'Krishna' means 'dark' or 'dark blue'. Draupadi plays with this overlap in semantics.

3. An ancient Hindu practice which literally means 'without union'. In this practice, a woman whose husband is either incapable of fathering a child or has died before she has had one would have sexual relations with another man solely for procreative purposes. This practice, allowed by *Manusmriti*, came with various clauses. The woman was prohibited from feeling sexual pleasure while sleeping with the man. Niyoga was seen as an act of dharma, practised in accordance with the will of god. The woman's husband would be considered the child's father and not the man she had slept with.

Source Tales

Alli

Exclusive to the Tamil, Dravidian tradition, the tale of Alli belongs more to oral and performative traditions than it does to textual ones. It is often sung as a ballad, performed as therukoothu (a form of street theatre) or narrated as villupattu (a form of musical storytelling). The Tamil phrase 'Alli Rajyam' (the reign of Alli) is used derogatorily to refer to households dominated by women.

Several versions of the ballad *Alli Arasani Malai* are in circulation.[7] Most Alli tales open with the childless Pandyan king temporarily entrusting his kingdom to a

---

[7] They range from the compositions of Pughazhendi Pulavar and Villiputurar in the Villupattu performance tradition to somewhat more contemporary ones, Pughazhendi, the sixteenth-century poet, also authored ballads narrating the Alli story. These include *Pavazhakkodi Malai, Pulandaran Kalava Malai* and *Eni Etram.* In the eighteenth century, Kappinipadi Pillai of Vellalur wrote *Alli Kadai.* In the early part of the twentieth century, a dramatic version of the tale called *Alli Natakam* was staged. It also went into print. In 2012, the ballad Alli Arasaani Maalai by the fifteenth-century poet Pugazhenthi was re-told by A.K. Perumal as *Arjunanin Tamizh Kadhaligal.*

man named Neenmugan (or Neelmugan). Hoping for a child, the king wanders the forests in search of a sage who can help him perform the putrakameshti yagna, a yagna believed to result in the birth of a child. To the king's great joy, he finds an infant girl hidden between the petals of a water lily. He names her Alli, after the flower. On his return to the kingdom, the king discovers to his shock that Neenmugan has usurped his throne. Acting on the advice of the sages, he returns to the forest and raises Alli like he would have a son. Alli is trained in warfare and soon becomes a skilled warrior. When she comes of age, she raises an army, attacks Neenmugan, stakes her claim to the throne and is eventually crowned queen of the Pandyan empire.[8] Alli earns for herself a considerable reputation as a fiercely independent warrior queen who refuses to marry.

Alli is the reigning queen of Madurai when the much-married Arjuna sets out with Krishna, his friend and spiritual guide, on a long pilgrimage from Mathura to Madurai.[9] The two are disguised as ascetics. In Madurai,

---

[8] In the *Alli Kadai* version, the Pandyan king seeks refuge with his father-in-law who, at the time, is ruling over a tiny principality and the vengeful Neenmugan declares war on the state, demanding tribute. Alli defies him and successfully leads the army against him and is subsequently crowned ruler of Madurai.

[9] The Alli–Arjuna story has interesting resonances with stories of Arjuna's exploits as narrated in the 'Arjunana Vanavasa Parva' of the Mahabharata. All the five Pandava brothers are married to Draupadi. They are bound by a contract to follow a system wherein Draupadi will spend a year with each of them in turn. If any one of

they meet an innkeeper (in some versions, a merchant), who describes to them Alli's valour and her triumph over Neenmugan. Arjuna wonders aloud if Alli is really a man dressed as a woman. The innkeeper proceeds to describe Alli's beauty and her qualities in great detail. He warns Arjuna that Alli is averse to men and to the idea of marriage. But Arjuna, unable to forget the picture that the man has painted of Alli's beauty, makes up his mind to possess her, one way or the other.

Disguised as women, Krishna and Arjuna meet Alli and eloquently describe to her Arjuna's valorous deeds and handsome looks. None of this impresses Alli however. Through a combination of force and trickery—the precise nature of which varies from version to version—Arjuna violates Alli. In the stage version, the tale concludes with Alli's marriage to Arjuna. Alli gracefully bows to him and

---

the Pandava brothers violates this arrangement, he would have to go into exile. A band of robbers abducts the cattle of a Brahmin who arrives at the Khandavaprastha court seeking Arjuna's help. It is only after Arjuna agrees to help him that he realises that his weapons are locked up in Yudhishtira's chamber. In fact, at that very moment, Yudhishtira is with Draupadi. After some hesitation, Arjuna ventures into Yudhishtira's chambers, retrieves his weapons, and sets off to help the Brahmin. He succeeds in restoring to the man his stolen cattle. When he returns, he volunteers to go on a twelve-year exile. Both Yudhishtira and Draupadi try to stop Arjuna, but the latter's mind is made up. He prepares himself for forest-life, and takes the vow of celibacy. Arjuna's vow does not last for long, though. During the course of his wanderings, Arjuna goes on to marry three women: Ulupi of the Naga kingdom, Chitrangada of Manipura and Subhadra of Dwaraka.

to his brothers as the gods shower their blessings on the newly wedded couple. However, the Alli of Pughazhendi Pulavar's narration steadfastly resists Arjuna's advances, even fighting a war with the Pandavas before ultimately capitulating.

Hidimbi

M.T. Vasudevan Nair's novel *Randamoozham* (translated from the Malayalam into English as *Bhima: Lone Warrior*),[10] portrays Bhima as a man whose love for and loyalty towards others goes largely unnoticed. Even Draupadi loves him less than she loves Arjuna. It is the Rakshasi Hidimbi alone who loves Bhima unreservedly.

After the Pandavas escape the burning house of lacquer, they wander incognito through a forest which happens to be the abode of the Rakshasa Hidimba and his sister Hidimbi. Bhima comes across a small pond filled with clear water. He drinks from it, and after a refreshing bath, attempts to fill some water in his upper garment to take back to the others. The water drips out almost instantly and Bhima hears a soft laugh from the bushes and a tribal woman (whom we are to soon learn is Hidimbi) emerges. It is telling that even in Bhima's description of Hidimbi, she appears more animal than human. Hidimbi

[10] M.T. Vasudevan Nair, *Bhima: Lone Warrior*, translated from the Malayalam by Gita Krishnankutty (New Delhi: HarperCollins, 2013).

falls in love with Bhima. Bhima slays her brother Hidimba and brings Hidimbi home to Kunti. Despite the selfless manner in which Hidimbi serves Kunti and the other Pandava brothers, she is always viewed with suspicion, perceived as less than human. When the Pandavas leave the forest for the village of Ekachakra, Hidimbi who is pregnant with Bhima's child is not allowed to accompany them. She raises their son Ghatotkacha on her own. Years later, Ghatotkacha is sent for so he can fight on the side of the Pandavas in the Kurukshetra war. He is eventually felled by Karna, who uses against him his lance Vyjayanthi, which he had reserved (as a last resort) for Arjuna. Karna no longer has a weapon to use against Arjuna. Ghatotkacha has essentially sacrificed his life to keep Arjuna safe.

Draupadi

Following the Kurukshetra war, Draupadi and the Pandavas embark on the last of their life journeys—an ascent of the Himalayas. Draupadi slips and falls en route. Of all her husbands, it is only Bhima who turns back to look. Yudhishtira forbids Bhima from walking back to Draupadi. As she lies dying, the Draupadi of Pratibha Ray's Oriya novel *Yajnaseni*[11] writes a letter to Krishna,

[11] Pratibha Ray, *Yajnaseni: The Story of Draupadi*, translated from the Oriya by Pradip Bhattacharya (New Delhi: Rupa, 1995). The novel is based on the Oriya Mahabharata by Sarala Das.

a letter in which she narrates the story of her difficult life beginning with her birth. Draupadi describes the yagna that her father King Drupad performed in order to get a son. She steps out of the sacrificial fire minutes after her twin brother Dhrishtadyumna, the daughter King Drupad hasn't been expecting, a daughter destined to change the very course of history. Draupadi is aware that she, like her brother, has been born to avenge her father's insult by Drona.[12] In Pratibha Ray's rendering, Draupadi is a scholar, a keen reader and a feisty poet.

Yajnaseni dwells on Draupadi's love for Krishna, a love which her favourite Sakhi Nitambini both teases and warns her about. Draupadi's love for Krishna is portrayed as more romantic than platonic. The novel thus departs from most mainstream versions of the Mahabharata in which the relationship between Draupadi and Krishna

---

[12] Drona, the son of a Brahmin and a master of archery, was a childhood friend of Drupada. Drupada promised Drona that he would give him half his kingdom when he ascended the throne. Drona got married and had a son named Ashwatthama. Feeling the pinch of poverty, Drona approached Drupada and reminded him of his promise. But Drupada said to him, 'What friendship can there be between a throned king and a wandering beggar? Friendship can only be between equals.' Drona vowed to avenge this insult. Years later, Arjuna, whom he had tutored in archery along with the other Pandavas and Kauravas, defeated Drupada and brought him to Drona. Drona took half of Drupada's kingdom and left him with the other half. 'We will now be equals,' he said. Drupada's most fervent wish was to avenge himself on Drona. He performs the yajna hoping to get a son who would help him avenge the insult.

is largely portrayed as platonic. When Draupadi finds herself, under rather unusual circumstances, wedded to all five of the Pandavas, she creates her own personal manifesto of chastity.

Yajnaseni also explores the dynamics and the long-standing tension between Draupadi and Karna which dates back to Draupadi's swayamvara and Karna's decision to participate in it and the humiliation he is subjected to because he is supposedly not of noble, royal birth. The novel also describes Draupadi's jealousy towards Krishna's sister, Subhadra, whom Arjuna abducts and marries. In her letter, Draupadi also writes of her humiliation and public disrobing at court.

Gandhari

In *Yuganta*,[13] a book of essays on the Mahabharata, Irawati Karve describes the young bride Gandhari's journey from Gandhara to Hastinapura. Gandhari is accompanied by a companion and by her brother Shakuni. The route is scenic and Gandhari's companion draws her attention to it. Won over by its beauty and charm, Shakuni decides to stay on in Hastinapura. When Gandhari's companion describes Shakuni's palace, pride fills Gandhari's heart at the thought of how prosperous her husband's family is. She wonders what it would be like to be queen of Hastinapura.

---

[13] Irawati Karve, *Yuganta: The End of an Epoch* (Hyderabad: Disha (Orient Longman), 1991).

That evening, her companion rushes into her chambers with the sobering news that her groom Dhritarashtra is blind. A shocked Gandhari swoons. When she regains consciousness, she decides to blindfold herself. She keeps the blindfold on almost to the end of her life.

After the devastating war in which Gandhari loses all her sons, she accompanies Dhritarashtra, Kunti and Vidura on their journey into the forest. Along the way, Dhritarashtra pleads with Gandhari to forgive him and his family for having kept her in the dark about his blindness and fervently implores her to remove her blindfold. Gandhari gives in and takes off the blindfold.

Kunti

The Kannada writer S.L. Bhyrappa's novel *Parva*[14] has neither gods nor superheroes, just ordinary human beings. The explanations for why the characters do what they do are rooted in human psychology, in cultural and historical circumstances. The novel is set in the twelfth century BCE. *Parva* offers an entirely rational explanation as to how Kunti and Madri conceive the Pandavas. There is no mention of Sage Kindama's curse which renders Pandu impotent nor of Sage Durvasa's boon thanks to which Kunti is able to invoke the gods and bear their

---

[14] S.L. Bhyrappa, *Parva*, translated from the Kannada by K. Raghavendra Rao (New Delhi: Sahitya Akademi, 1994).

children.[15] What we do know is that Pandu is incapable of fathering a child. Anxious to produce an heir to the throne before his brother Dhritarashtra does so, he persuades Kunti to enter into niyoga with members of a clan called the Devas. Her only goal must be to conceive sons by them and as soon as that goal is attained she must return to Pandu. The Devas belong to Gangadvara, a land surrounded by mountains. Theirs is a far freer society and their ideas about sexuality and marriage are radically different from those of the Kshatriyas. Yudhishtira is born of Kunti's union with the Dharmaraja, a man from the Deva clan. Pandu feels he is not as strong as a son of the Kuru lineage ought to be and attributes this weakness to the fact that Dharmaraja isn't a warrior. He instructs

[15] In the *Sambhava Parva* of Vyasa's *Mahabharata*, the Kuru prince Pandu goes hunting one day and happens to see a stag mating with a doe. The stag is actually the sage Kindama and the doe his wife, but Pandu, who does not know this, shoots an arrow at the stag, wounding him fatally. A dying Kindama curses Pandu to a life of celibacy. If Pandu were to ever give in to lust, he would die while in the act of making love. Sage Durvasa gives Kunti a boon in the form of a divine mantra. In order to invoke a god of her choice and conceive a child by him, all Kunti has to do was to utter the mantra. It is this mantra which Kunti employs as a young woman in order to invoke the sun god Surya, resulting in the out-of-wedlock birth of Karna. In the *Sambhava Parva*, Pandu instructs Kunti to use the divine mantra and invoke the gods, so she can conceive and bear children for him. Yudhisthira is born of Kunti's union with Dharma, Bhima of her union with Vayu and Arjuna of her union with Indra. With Kunti's help, Madri is able to invoke the two Ashvinis. Of Madri's union with the Ashvinis are born Nakula and Sahadeva.

Kunti to sleep with Maruta, the army chieftain of the Devas, so she can bear him a son who has the strength of a warrior. Kunti finds herself falling deeply in love with Maruta, who returns her love in equal measure. When she becomes pregnant with Bhima, she must part from Maruta.

References

Bharath Kumar and Srilata K. (trans), 'The Ballad of Alli' (unpublished). Source text: A.K. Perumal's *Arjunanin Tamizh Kadhaligal* (based on the play *Alli Arasaani Maalai* by the fifteenth-century poet Pugazhenthi).

S.L. Bhyrappa, *Parva*, translated from the Kannada by K. Raghavendra Rao (New Delhi: Sahitya Akademi, 1994).

Bibek Debroy, *The Mahabharata*, Books 1 to 10 (New Delhi: Penguin, 2015).

Chitra Banerjee Divakaruni, *The Palace of Illusions* (New York: Doubleday, 2008).

Irawati Karve, *Yuganta: The End of an Epoch* (Hyderabad: Disha (Orient Longman), 1991).

M.T. Vasudevan Nair, *Bhima: Lone Warrior*, translated from the Malayalam by Gita Krishnankutty (New Delhi: HarperCollins, 2013).

A.K. Perumal, *Arjunanin Tamizhaga Kaadhaligal* (Nagercoil: Kalachuvadu Publications, 2012 (based on the play *Alli Arasaani Maalai* by the fifteenth-century poet Pugazhenthi).

Vijaya Ramaswamy, 'From "Amazonian" Warrior to Submissive Wife: The Taming of Alli', *Economic and*

Political Weekly, Vol. 41, No. 17 (29 April–5 May 2006), pp. 1661–1668.

Pratibha Ray, *Yajnaseni: The Story of Draupadi*, translated from the Oriya by Pradip Bhattacharya (New Delhi: Rupa, 1995).

V.S. Sukthankar, *The Mahabharata* (Adiparvan), Vol. I (Pune: Bhandarkar Oriental Research Institute, 1933).

Wendy Doniger, 'The Mahabharata: A Text for All Seasons', Foreword to Carole Satyamurti's *Mahabharata: A Modern Retelling* (New York: Norton, 2015).

Acknowledgements

This Foundation Project is implemented by India Foundation for the Arts (IFA) under the Arts Practice programme, made possible with support from Sony Pictures Entertainment Fund.

Grateful thanks to:

V.K. Karthika for the hand-holding and the thoughtful edits. Without her, this wouldn't be the book it is.

Team Westland for their commitment to literature.

India Foundation for the Arts for funding the research that went into the writing of this book. Special thanks to Arundhati Ghosh, Menaka Rodriguez, Sumana Chandrasekhar and Mridupankhi Rajkumari.

Sangam House for a residency at the Jamun, Bangalore where I first ventured into these waters. Arshia Sattar for dreaming up Sangam House.

The Bhandarkar Oriental Research Institute, Pune for generous access to important source material and to scholarly lectures on the Mahabharata as part of their online course '18 Parvans of the Mahabharata'.

Geethanjali Rajan for lessons in haikai.

Fióna Bolger for reading every word of a messy first draft, for her very helpful suggestions and edits.

Arundhathi Subramaniam for the gift of her attention, for her incisive comments on structure and form.

Karthika Naïr for going over my poems with a poet's eye and for her wise and astute feedback.

Ranjit Hoskote for being my first reader.

Priya Sarukkai Chabria for featuring poems from the sequences in *Poetry at Sangam.*

Bharath Kumar for research support and for the work on Alli.

Azhagarasan for lending me his Alli books.

Kavya Bharati for giving my Hidimbi poems their first home.

Premila Paul and Ganesh Babu of SCILET, Madurai for tomato rice, tall, iced glasses of jigarthanda and guided tours of the Meenakshi temple.

Shobhana Kumar, Fióna Bolger, Anne Tannam and Alvy Carraghar for being my community.

Vatsala, Mani, Aniruddha and Ananya without whom none of this would have been possible.

Praise for the Book

'Words dripping with desire and longing, words weighed down by grief and betrayal, words so tender and fragrant with love: K. Srilata's *Footnotes to the Mahabharata* is filled with gems that leave the reader staring at a blank wall every few minutes.'

—Akila Kannadasan in *The Hindu*

'Srilata's poems allow us to revisit women's lives in the Mahabharata, reminding us of the contemporaneity of ancient myths and stories. The speaking women in these poems display a fierce intelligence through pain, anguish and pleasure.'

—Ratna Raman in *The Tribune*

'*Footnotes* [*to the Mahabharata*] succeeds in seamlessly fusing the narrative modes of the epic with the poignancy of the lyric and in valorously inserting a feminist ethics in historical discourse. Without raising a rant or an accusation, it speaks with the confidence of facts, lived experience, and retrospective clarity ... Srilata writes with an aching lyricism, a lilt that captures the cadence of Tamil Sangam poetry and the polish of contemporary English idiom.'

—Basudhara Roy in *The Bangalore Review*

'Srilata's collection skilfully weaves the lives of these five women [from the Mahabharata] into a single string and lets them break free ... The poems remind us that had [the women] been free to speak, their words would have shattered the kingdom.'

—Kabir Deb in *Outlook*

'The most compelling voice in the collection belongs to young Draupadi—passionate, poetic, and feisty—whose "life of the mind" is already a cause for concern for her parents. Rejecting all feminine ornamentation, she dons an ascetic look befitting a scholar until she becomes love-crazed, pining for Krishna.'

—Iswarya V. in *Frontline*